Women of the Bible
Volume 5

Carnal & Conniving

by  W9-ART-309

Shirley M. Starr

ISBN   0-9728162-5-9

First Printing   October, 2005

NOTE: All Bible references taken from
The Authorized Version (KJV).

Printed in the U.S.A. by
Morris Publishing
3212 East Highway 30
Kearney, NE 68847
1-800-650-7888

Dedication

This book is dedicated
to the ladies who
participated in the
early home Bible studies:

Nora Petrie, Audrey Fritz,
Marie Setzler, Kathy Foster,
LeAnn Brown, and Gayle Barton

and

to my enthusiastic
and faithful proofreader
Joanna Allen

♥ Thank you for contributing to these works! ♥

Preface

Carnal and Conniving! These are character traits we would not seek or pursue. However, even as Christian ladies, we often battle the flesh in these areas. Emotional as we are, we often seek to take matters into our own hands, hoping situations will turn out "just right" as **we** foresee! Our impatience and impulsiveness motivate us to act and not to wait.

The Apostle Paul faced this battle with the flesh and the spirit. In Romans 7:15-25, he describes his struggle with this issue: *"For that which I do I allow not: for what I would, that do I not; but what I hate, that do I. . . For I know that in me (that is, in my flesh,) dwelleth no good thing: for to will is present with me; but how to perform that which is good I find not. . .I find then a law, that, when I would do good, evil is present with me. . ."*

The ladies in this volume faced that same raging battle, but were miserably defeated. They did not apply the solution the Apostle later shared in Galatians 5:16: *"Walk in the Spirit, and ye shall not fulfil the lust of the flesh."* Instead, they resorted to carnal weapons, refusing to bring into captivity "every thought to the obedience of Christ." *(2 Corinthians 10:4)* Many of them suffered spiritual and even physical death due to their actions, fulfilling Romans 8:7: *"For to be carnally minded is death; but to be spiritually minded is life and peace."*

May these ladies of the past be a motivating force, encouraging to us to walk after the Spirit, to be spiritually minded, and to seek life and peace.

Table of Contents

Women of the Bible, Volume 5
Carnal & Conniving

Title page
Copyright page
Dedication page
Preface

Chapter 1

LOT'S WIFE

"The Material-Minded Woman"
"The Frozen Face"
"No Time For Angels"

Facts

Husband:	Lot
Children:	Four daughters
Occupation:	Housewife

Background

(Gen. 13:10-13, 14:12, Luke 17:32)

What can we possibly learn from Lot's wife? The Old Testament cites only fifteen words about her. However, the Lord thought she was important enough to include in the New Testament in the second shortest verse in the Bible, with a warning at that: "Remember Lot's wife."

Oddly enough, her **name** is never mentioned anywhere in the Bible, although we do learn some great lessons from her life and actions.

How did it all begin? Abraham gave Lot first choice of the land in the area. When Lot saw the well-watered plains of Jordan, he knew it was the perfect territory for his flocks and herds. In the beginning, he pitched his tent toward Sodom. We see he had a tent without an altar, and no mention is ever made of Lot building an altar and having family worship. We hear nothing of his wife at this stage. Was he married when he chose Sodom or did he perhaps meet his wife there? There is no record of her trying to prevent Lot's choice. Did she encourage him to move into Sodom? Did she use her power of influence? We will never know for sure, but eventually, the family moved right into Sodom.

Materialism

(Gen. 13:5-6; 19:1; Luke 17:28-31; Ezek. 16:49-50)

We know she had a rich husband. Abram and Lot had so many flocks, herds, and tents that the land could not contain them, forcing them to split up. Wealth was measured in flocks and herds, and Genesis 13:6 says "their substance was great. . ."

Not only did she have a rich husband, but she had an important husband. He "sat in the gate of Sodom." *(Gen. 19:1)* What was so important about sitting in the gate? The gate was the center of public activity in the city. John R. Rice in his *Genesis* commentary reveals the following things about the gate:

1. People met their friends at the gate.
2. People shared their news at the gate.
3. People traded their goods at the gate.
4. People carried on legal transactions at the gate, such as making marriage contracts, proclamations, etc.

Since the gate was a center of bustling activity and city life, a lot of gossip was probably exchanged there. Perhaps Lot was involved in the city political scene, and perhaps his wife was a city councilman's wife.

It seems that her gods may have been money, possessions, and social prestige. How do we know this? Luke 17:28 says that in the days of Lot, they ate, drank, bought, sold, planted, and builded. Perhaps she lived for material things. This is a vivid warning to us not to become so enamored by shopping, buying, selling, building, etc. We can spend so much time on these things that there is no time left for serving God, keeping our homes, training our children, or caring for our husbands. Mrs.

Lot's heart seemed to be turned this way, as she was unwilling to sacrifice and live with less to serve the God of Heaven.

Ezekiel 16:49 says the iniquity of Sodom was "pride, fulness of bread, and **abundance of idleness**." The people did nothing to help the poor and needy. Too much food and ease can ruin a person. Remember the old adage: "an idle mind is the devil's workshop"? We need to stay busy for the Lord, making Him the priority of our lives. Paul said he made himself servant to all that he might gain the more. *(1 Cor. 9:19)* Even Jesus "took upon him the form of a servant." *(Phil. 2:7)* There should never be an "abundance of idleness" in our lives. Besides being a servant to our families, there are many needy people to serve also. There is always someone needing a helping hand, a friendly smile, or a word of encouragement.

Ezekiel 16:50 goes on to say that the Sodomites "were haughty and committed abomination." This is the kind of environment which surrounded Lot and his family.

Warning (Gen. 19:1-8, 12-17; 2 Pet. 2:6-8)

One evening, as Lot sat in the gate, he saw two angels passing by. Showing hospitality, he invited them to spend the night. They declined, saying they would sleep in the street. He greatly urged them, and they finally agreed. Being a good host, Lot cooked for them. Where were his wife and daughters? Remember Abraham and Sarah? They worked together serving their guests. Had Lot's wife taught her daughters to serve? Did she have a servant's heart herself? Or did Lot just enjoy cooking as some men do?

Even though Lot was a "just" man, his thinking had become carnal. Before the family was ready to retire, the men of the city circled the house round about. They asked Lot to bring out his angel guests so they could "know" them. They meant "know" them in a sexual sense, showing how perverted the people of Sodom had become. The men of Sodom were homosexuals. Lot offered his own daughters to the men in place of the angels, and we see no intervention from his wife here. Where was she? Why did she remain silent? How did he become so twisted in his thinking? (Perhaps it resulted from his constant contact with this wicked crowd.)

The angels instructed Lot to get his family out of the city, as the Lord was going to destroy it. However, Lot had no witness or testimony with his own sons-in-law and they refused to heed his warning. Lot and his family had fellowshipped too long with the ungodly until his family had just come to accept their perversion as the norm. Second Peter 2:6-8 says Lot had been vexed daily "with their unlawful deeds." Why had he remained in Sodom? Why didn't he practice the principle of separation? The family had become so entrenched in Sodom and Gomorrah's life-style that the angels had to physically lay hold of them to get them to leave. They were warned not to look back or to camp close to the area, but were instructed to escape all the way to the mountain.

Half-Heartedness

(Gen. 19:26; 1 Kings 18:21; Matt 6:24; 10:37; Luke 9:62, 14:26, 16:13, 17:32-33; Jam. 1:8)

Genesis 19:26 continues with the sad part of the story. Lot's wife had a divided mind. She faced salvation but refused to go forward. The angel had even laid hold of her hand, but Scripture says she disobeyed, looked back, and became a pillar of salt. Why did she hesitate? Was she thinking,

> Why should I leave my home? Living in this city, in this
> house, is good, is it not? I am familiar with everything.
> My husband has an honorable position on the city council,
> and my daughters are engaged to be married. Life is taking
> its natural course as usual. Nothing has really changed. Why
> should God's judgment suddenly come on us now?
>
> *(Karssen, Book 2, pp. 32-33)*

Carnal and Conniving
Women of the Bible, volume 5

Being unwilling to lose material things and save her life, she lost **both** in the end. Amazingly, like some of the other women we have read about, she is mentioned in the New Testament. Christ thought her example was important enough to include in Luke 17:32-33 and warns us to "remember Lot's wife."

What kind of penalties did she face for being double-minded?

1. **Indecision** – She tried to have the best of both worlds and lost both. We see this problem in 1 Kings 18:21 when Elijah asked the Israelites how long they would halt between two opinions. James 1:8 tells us "a double-minded man is unstable in all his ways." What an accurate description of Lot's wife and a warning to us as ladies to have our priorities right! We are not to become so entangled with our homes, security, materialism, and prestige that we are unable to obey the Lord!

2. **Loss of Influence** – She was unable to progress spiritually when looking at the world. Christ puts a high price on discipleship and says in Luke 9:62 that "no man, having put his hand to the plow, and **looking back**, is fit for the kingdom of God." Our love for Him is to be so great that our love for our families will seem as hate in comparison. *(Luke 14:26)* Because Lot's wife did not have this kind of love for the Lord, she did not have a spiritually positive influence.

3. **Disaster** – She refused to take the chance of a new start. Often we fear change; we fear the unknown. But God has promised to be with us through those changing seasons of our lives. And usually the change is for the better and not the worse. God often uses change to mold and make our lives, to make us stronger, and to make us better equipped to help others. But she refused that change and met with disaster.

Carnal and Conniving
Women of the Bible, volume 5

Lot's wife was not just struck dead, but turned into a pillar of salt as a memorial. Could that pillar of salt be a reminder to us of the salt that never got into Sodom? "Ye are the salt of the earth: but if the salt have lost his savour, wherewith shall it be salted? It is thenceforth good for nothing, but to be cast out, and to be trodden under foot of men." *(Matt. 5:13)*

Effects
(Gen. 19:8, 14, 32-36; Prov. 14:1, 11; 1 Cor. 15:33)

Once again we see the effects of sin on others. Her sin not only affected her, but the lives of her family. What a pit they had sunk into! Two of the daughters had married men of low character who were not saved from destruction and refused to heed their father-in-law's word! *(Gen. 19:14)*

Lot and the two unmarried daughters who escaped with him did not build an altar to thank God for saving them. No gratefulness was expressed! We see they were delivered from Sodom, but Sodom was still in their hearts. The daughters had their father drink wine and then committed incest with him! How could they even think of doing such a thing?

First Corinthians 15:33 says, "Be not deceived: evil communications corrupt good manners." Their years in Sodom had taken a toll on them spiritually. They had been corrupted by the constant environment of sin. Could their mother's presence have prevented this? Proverbs 14:11 says, "The house of the wicked shall be overthrown: but the tabernacle of the upright shall flourish." It appears that Lot's wife left her daughters no spiritual heritage. "Every wise woman buildeth her house: but the foolish plucketh it down with her hands." *(Prov. 14:1)*

Conclusions

Lot's wife was "riding the fence." Are you "riding the fence" in your spiritual life – trying to have the best of both worlds? Is your life carnal, taken up with money, possessions, and social prestige? Lot's wife was dominated by the thought of "what used to be." Do your memories have you bound? Memories are important, but we must not be chained to the past. While we dwell on the past, we are crippled to face the present.

Are you in a rut in your spiritual life and refusing to move forward? What is the next step for you – baptism, Bible reading, faithful church attendance, tithing? Perhaps you have not yet even taken the first step of salvation.

Lot's wife was a poor witness and had no souls to take with her out of Sodom besides her two daughters. How about you? Are you witnessing for the Lord? Are you taking folks to church with you?

Once again we see the woman's power of influence being squandered. Remember this trait can be used for good or bad, and it was wasted in the life of Lot's wife. What an opportunity she had, but she neglected to take advantage of it! Her family, friends, and neighbors suffered because of her negligence.

Families suffer when parents live for themselves, and this seemed to be the case in the Lot family. We are responsible to steer our families in the right direction. Are you leaving your family a spiritual heritage? Are you like the wise woman who builds her house up or are you a foolish woman who tears it down with her own hands?

There is always a price to pay for disobedience. Lot's wife disobeyed when she looked back. She looked back to the "good old days" just like the Israelites looked back to Egypt and the leeks, the onions, and the garlic. Paul said he forgot those things which were behind and reached forth unto those things which were before. *(Phil. 3:13)* What a tragedy that Lot's wife refused to follow the same principle and did not "press toward the mark for the prize of the high calling of God in Christ Jesus." *(Phil. 3:14)* What a shame that she could not keep "looking unto Jesus, the author and finisher of our faith. . ." *(Heb. 12:2)*

Don't look back! Remember Lot's wife!

Lot's Wife's Roles

1. Wife
2. Mother
3. Mother-in-law

Lot's Wife's Character Traits

1. Self-centeredness
2. Stubbornness
3. Reluctance
4. Half-heartedness
5. Foolishness
6. Indecisiveness
7. Double-mindedness

Chapter 2

REBEKAH
"The Deceiver"
"The Lady in Mid-Life Crisis"

Facts

Husband:	Isaac
Children:	Jacob, Esau
Occupation:	Housewife
Her name means:	"Tie rope," "Noose," "Captivating"

Background

(Gen. 22:23; 24:1-61)

This romantic account opens with Abraham sending his trusted servant, Eliezer, to seek a bride for his son, Isaac. Abraham had Eliezer promise not to take a daughter of the Canaanites, but to return to Mesopotamia and take a bride for Isaac from Abraham's own kindred. Eliezer explicitly obeyed his master and asked the Lord to send a damsel who not only would give him a drink, but would water his camels also.

Shortly after his prayer, Rebekah, daughter of Bethuel, Abraham's nephew, approached the well with her pitcher upon her shoulder. A routine event (drawing water) was about to become part of a divine plan for her life. Scripture tells us that she was very pretty, appealing, and chaste. She lived up to her name meaning "captivating." Men may have been spellbound by her beauty. Demonstrating kindness, courtesy, and ambition, she drew water for Eliezer to drink, saying she would draw water for the camels also. Genesis 24:10 tells us Eliezer had taken ten camels with him. That is a lot of water to draw! Rebekah did not hesitate, but demonstrated a real servant's heart and proceeded to do just as she had said. It has been estimated that she perhaps drew 30-60 gallons of water for the camels to drink! It appears that she was a lady accustomed to hard work and going the "extra mile."

Asking whose daughter she was, Eliezer gave her gifts of a golden earring and two bracelets. Rebekah remained poised, tactful, and gracious, even inviting him to lodge at her father's house.

Running home, she told her family the happenings of the day. They communicated well with one another. Her brother, Laban, ran out to meet Eliezer. We do not see her father mentioned anywhere.

Her family opened their home to Eliezer, and he explained the whole reason for his visit. The family agreed to let Rebekah go to become Isaac's bride, but the next morning requested that she remain for ten more days. Eliezer asked them not to hinder him and to let her go now. They asked Rebekah what she wished to do. Not hesitating at all, she said, "I will go." Notice that there was no arranged marriage without her assent. Parents and daughter discussed it and agreed.

What a woman of decision and adventure she was, showing courage and spirit. She was willing to marry a man she had never seen, willing to leave her comfort zone and convenient lifestyle. She chose to leave family and friends, travel to a strange land, and marry a strange man. She would not have a big wedding, a shower, or friends and family to see her start her newly married life! The family agreed to the arrangement, not knowing when or if they would ever see her again.

What a beautiful picture of the church age – Abraham (~God) sending his servant Eliezer (~Holy Spirit) to fetch a bride, Rebekah (~the church), for Isaac, his son (~Jesus).

Romance and Marriage   (Gen. 24:62-67; 25:20-28)

One of the most romantic scenes in the Bible occurs in Genesis 24:62-67. Can you imagine Isaac's eagerness to meet this woman who was to become his wife? He had probably become very lonely since his mother's death three years before. Scripture tells us he was forty years old at the time of the marriage. Picture Rebekah's nervousness and anticipation in meeting the man who would become her life partner. Isaac loved Rebekah and was comforted by her. Everything was perfect, or so it seemed.

One thing however marred their happiness. Rebekah was barren. Isaac was a man of prayer and entreated the Lord on her behalf. The Lord heard and answered, and Rebekah conceived. Imagine the happiness of the couple, expecting their first baby! Little did she know that she would be the first lady to have twins! As the children struggled within her, she went to inquire of the Lord. This is the first record of a woman making an appeal to God. We notice that she and Isaac did not pray together over this.

Isaac was sixty years old when the twin boys were born. They had waited twenty years to have children. Imagine the excitement and joy in their home! Their schedule surely changed with two new babies on the scene. We see them making their first drastic mistake. They showed favoritism to the new little boys. Isaac loved Esau and Rebekah loved Jacob. *(Gen. 25:28)* Great turmoil would come into their home because of this fatal error.

Trial and Tribulation   (Gen. 26:1-11, 34-35)

The first trial which arose in their home after the birth was a famine in the land. Isaac went to Gerar, probably to garner food and help for his family. However, we see him repeating the same mistake that his father Abraham had made. He lied to the men, telling them Rebekah was his sister. Abimelech, a heathen Philistine king, rebuked him for it. God protected them in spite of themselves and their sin. How embarrassing that God would have to use a heathen to rebuke a believer!

The next trial that beset the Isaac family was Esau's marriage to a Hittite woman. Perhaps they had dreams of their son marrying a godly lady, someone who held their beliefs and values. In their minds' eye, they could picture grandchildren nearby to love and spoil, family get-togethers, and sweet fellowship. However, their dreams were dashed! Scripture says this was a grief of mind to Isaac and Rebekah. Had their favoritism driven Esau to rebellion? Beware of favoritism. Were Isaac and Rebekah talking things out along the way, or as they aged, were they drifting farther and farther apart?

Favoritism and Deception (Gen. 27:1-17, 41-46; Prov.14:1, 31:12)

Rebekah's personality now took on a great change. Perhaps she was experiencing menopause or mid-life crisis. On the other hand, she may have been a fatigued care-giver as we see Isaac's failing health. Whatever the case, we see three things happening to her:

1. She had poor communication with Isaac.
2. She had seemingly lost respect for Isaac.
3. She centered all of her ambitions on Jacob.

Isaac had become an obstacle to her because he loved Esau. Esau was an obstacle, because as the oldest son he would receive all the blessings and inheritance she wanted Jacob to have. Favoritism was about to take its toll.

Rebekah eavesdropped on Isaac and Esau's conversation. She heard Isaac requesting Esau to bring him some savory meat and promising to bless Esau. She faced her hour of temptation and began to connive. Her power of influence was about to be used to inflict an unjust deed.

Taking the reins of the whole family into her own hands, Rebekah showed her favoritism and planned how Jacob could receive his father's blessing instead of Esau. What happens when a woman does this?

1. It destroys the home. *(Prov. 14:1)*
2. It forces children to hate. *(Gen. 27:41)*
3. It hinders the husband's response to God.

What happened to the young Rebekah we knew with all of the great character qualities? Had she maintained her walk with God? What would make her stoop to lying and deception? What happened to her kind and submissive spirit, her servant's heart? She was ready to sow to the wind and reap the whirlwind. *(Hosea 8:7)* What an admonition to us to maintain a close, daily walk with the Lord, to have a hedge of Scripture in our minds and hearts as a protection against Satan's devices. *(2 Cor. 2:11)* Just because we have walked near to God in the past does not mean we always will. The flesh fights against the Spirit daily. We **must** maintain our walk with God.

Perhaps she felt Isaac was making a drastic mistake. However, she ran ahead of God, did not give her expectations over to God, and did not wait upon Him or seek His will. Are we afraid to let our husbands fail; can't God handle it? Can't we give them room to grow through their mistakes? Can't we trust God to work in their lives?

With Isaac's health failing, Rebekah probably became insecure and felt she had to start taking control. She most likely reasoned that she would be better taken care of if her favorite son, Jacob, had the birthright. She became sharp and cunning and began to give orders. She had determined what she was going to do, regardless of the consequences. Genesis 27:13 says she was even willing to assume full responsibility for her actions. One sin led to another, and she even stole Esau's clothing. Remember, Esau was a married man at this time, so she was interfering in his household, too!

The deed was committed, and Isaac mistakenly blessed Jacob instead of Esau. Rebekah had taught her son to lie! What hate, anger, and confusion there was in this Christian home. Esau purposed in his heart to kill Jacob. Now what would Rebekah do?

Perhaps she thought she was doing God's will, as Genesis 25:23 says the "elder shall serve the younger." God had given her this prophecy during her pregnancy. Perhaps she was trying to accomplish the will of God in a fleshly manner. Facing contradictory forces, she did not let God help her integrate them. Like Sarah, she moved on her emotions and did not wait for God to intervene. She drove a wedge between her two sons that would last for years to come! Continuing to practice deceit and wanting to protect Jacob, she skillfully persuaded Isaac to allow Jacob to leave, saying that he might marry Hittite women like Esau did. This is the last communication we see in Scripture between Isaac and Rebekah. What a sad ending to such a perfect beginning!

Consequences and Effects
(Gen. 27:19-20, 24; 49:31; Rom. 3:8; 9:10-12)

Rebekah sacrificed four things by her actions. She got what she wanted but lost what she had. Can anything good come out of doing evil? She lost:

1. **Jacob's presence**, ie., what she loved most. He wandered for twenty years. She never saw her thirteen grandchildren, dying before Jacob ever returned.
2. **Isaac's love**
3. **Esau's respect** – She had to face him every day.
4. **Peace of soul**

She wanted her own way and moved on her emotions, even teaching her son to lie. She was mentally and emotionally unfaithful to Isaac, and we do not ever see her apologizing. Although she had physical beauty, she lacked the beauty of godly character. What a great beginning; what a sad ending! She is a prime example of sowing and reaping.

We hear no more of Rebekah after her sin. Romans 9:10 does mention her and the twins' conception by Isaac, once again confirming an Old Testament lady in the New Testament. She was buried in Machpelah alongside Abraham and Sarah.

Amazingly, God still demonstrated His great mercy toward her. Though Rebekah did not live to see it, Jacob became the father of the twelve tribes, and Joseph stood out as a godly grandson.

Lessons and Warnings

We can learn many lessons from Rebekah's life. Though we may start out with a good beginning, we are still prone to sin. First Peter 5:8 warns us to "be sober, be vigilant; because your adversary the devil, as a roaring lion, walketh about, seeking whom he may devour." First Corinthians 10:12 also warns us: "Wherefore let him that thinketh he standeth take heed lest he fall." The Christian life is a race and an ongoing battle. Just because we start out great does not mean we can become lax. We need to maintain a close relationship with our Lord and Saviour to receive His "Well Done."

Rebekah's sin affected the whole family, just like Eve's, Sarah's, Hagar's, and Lot's wife's. We are not an island unto ourselves and will stand and give account someday to an Almighty God.

Sin's consequences take the joy out of life. Rebekah never saw her thirteen grandchildren. There were no family reunions for this family! She had broken every happy relationship she had.

Carnal and Conniving
Women of the Bible, volume 5

Godly character is more important than physical beauty. Though Rebekah had outer beauty, she lacked continuous inner beauty. Are you spending more time on physical beauty than on maintaining godly character? Do you spend more time in front of the mirror on your physical appearance than you do in the mirror of God's Word? *(James 1)* What is top priority in your life? Is it shopping, friends, home and children, or inner growth and godly character?

Several warnings ring out to us from Rebekah's life:

1. Do not seek success at the cost of truth.
2. Do not let children make your relationship with your husband deteriorate. What will you have when the children leave home?
3. Avoid favoritism at all costs. Be equitable to all of your children.
4. Remain faithful to your husband and keep him number one. Do not side with the children against him. Let him make the final decisions.
5. Maintain communication with your husband.
6. Do not let midlife turn you into a conniving, bitter woman.
7. Do not take your husband's responsibilities into your hands.

Rebekah's Roles

1. Wife
2. Mother
3. Servant
4. Deceiver
5. Conniver
6. Schemer
7. Thief
8. Comforter

Rebekah's Character Traits

1. Ambition
2. Decisiveness
3. Courage
4. Poise
5. Tactfulness
6. Graciousness
7. Bias
8. Deceitfulness

Chapter 3

ZIPPORAH

"The Rebellious Wife"
"The Woman Who Wrongly Opposed Her Husband"

Facts

Husband:	Moses
Children:	Gershom, Eliezer
Occupation:	Housewife, Shepherdess
Her name means:	"Bird," "A little sparrow"

Background (Ex. 2:16-20; 3:1; 18:1)

Zipporah was the daughter of Jethro, a priest of Midian. Did this make her a preacher's child? Scripture makes no mention of her mother, so we have no record of how her mother may have influenced her life.

Zipporah, along with her six other sisters, was watering their father's sheep. Moses had fled from Egypt to the desert and met this group of young ladies at the well. Other shepherds were there as well and tried to drive the girls away. Coming to their rescue, Moses courteously helped them water their flock.

After returning home, their father asked them how they had finished their work so early that day. They told their father how an Egyptian had helped them draw water for the animals and for themselves. The father told them to call the man and invite him to eat bread with them.

Marriage and Motherhood (Ex. 2:21-2; 18:3-4)

Moses met the family and was content to live there. Scripture does not share how the romance began (like it does with Isaac and Rebekah or Jacob and Rachel), but Jethro finally ended up giving Zipporah, his daughter, as a wife to Moses. We do not see any evidence that Moses sought God about the matter. Did he perhaps step out of God's will by marrying a Gentile?

Zipporah became the mother of two sons, Gershom and Eliezer. Gershom means "a stranger," and Eliezer means "God is help." Unlike other Bible women we have read about, Zipporah was an undistinguished wife and is mentioned only three times by name in Scripture.

Return to Egypt (Gen. 17:10-14; Ex. 4:19-26)

Moses worked for his father-in-law and took care of the flock on the backside of the desert. One day as he was going about his usual chores, God appeared to him in a burning bush and instructed him to return to Egypt and help deliver the people from the terrible bondage in which they suffered.

Moses approached Jethro, his father-in-law and asked for permission to return to Egypt. He had been gone for forty years! Just think—forty years of not seeing his family! Jethro gave his blessing to Moses, so Moses gathered his wife and sons and set out on the journey.

However, Moses had some unfinished business with the Lord. On the way to Egypt, he became ill. Scripture says the "Lord met him and sought to kill him." Why? Hadn't God asked him to return to Egypt? It appears that Moses had neglected to circumcise his son. The father usually performed this ceremony on the eighth day after the child's birth. Everyone not circumcised broke the covenant. Moses had sinned in failing to do this.

Carnal and Conniving

Perhaps Zipporah did not share Moses' spiritual values and was indulgent of the child, not wanting to see the boy put through the painful process. We see no expression of her faith in the Biblical account. Unlike other Bible women dedicated to God, we never see her praying or seeking God on behalf of anything. Had Moses compromised with her to keep peace in the family? Remember, Moses was unequally yoked.

Apparently Moses was so ill that Zipporah circumcised the child. Or did she just take matters into her own hands and finally agree in a fit of rage? We can only speculate. However, the command was finally carried out, but Zipporah was not happy about it! It is at this point that we find the only words spoken by her in Scripture. Appearing to be in rebellion, she reproached Moses and called him a "bloody husband."

The Lord "let Moses go" and lifted the illness from him. Matthew Henry says, "When we return to God in a way of duty, He will return to us in a way of mercy." *(Henry, Vol. 1, p. 290)* We are only happy when we are living in obedience to His commands.

Separation from Moses <small>(Ex. 18:1-7)</small>

From Exodus 18:1-2, it seems that Moses sent Zipporah back to Midian to her father. We do not know if this was before or after the plagues; however, we never see her in Egypt with him during the period of the plagues. Why did he send her back?

1. So his family would not meet the discouragements of the plagues?
2. So his family would not be a hindrance to him? An unbelieving wife could never handle the trials to come.

It seems that Zipporah may have caused a rift in their relationship and interfered with her husband's spiritual leadership. We do not see her being a helpmeet at the most crucial point of Moses' life, that of delivering the Israelites. In fact, we do not see her playing any major role in Moses' life after this episode.

The last time she is mentioned in the Scriptures is when her father and sons re-join Moses. *(Ex. 18:2-6)* Exodus 18:7 shows Moses greeting his father-in-law, but no mention is made of the reunion with Zipporah. How would a normal man and wife act after being separated for a period of time? They would be anxious and probably run into each other's arms. We see no contact between her and Moses during this reunion.

Conclusions
(Ex. 18:10-12; 1 Sam. 15:23; Psa. 62:5; 2 Cor. 6:14; Gal. 6:7; Eph. 5:24)

We see only a sad ending to what could have been a happy life. Zipporah seemed to be a prejudiced and rebellious wife. We do not even know if she lived long enough to raise her two sons. Did she leave a spiritual legacy for her family like Jochebed did? We do know she did not experience the exodus or see God's mighty hand of deliverance on behalf of the Israelites. She was not the helpmeet Moses needed to lead the complaining Israelites. We will see Moses' sister, Miriam, as a leader of the women. A happy part of the story is that Jethro finally did believe on Moses' God. This fact is evidenced by his saying: "Now I know that the Lord is greater than all gods. . ." *(Ex. 18:11)* Following this, he offered a burnt offering and sacrifices to God.

Though Zipporah's life is not discussed in any detail in the Bible, we can glean some important lessons. When we reject our husband's authority, we are really rejecting God and a special gift He has given to us. Why do so many women want to run the home and make all of the decisions? God knows women are not emotionally strong enough to handle it. After all, He made us! Therefore, in His great wisdom and knowledge, He gave us the command in Ephesians 5:24 to be subject to our husbands. Being subject does not mean being a slave. It means being lovingly obedient to our husbands.

Perhaps Zipporah had urged Moses to compromise and not circumcise his son. God hates compromise. By getting our husbands to compromise, we devalue and demean their God-given role, making them even less effective. Why do we do this? Because we are afraid they will fail, or it will mean a change in our own life that we do not want to make. Psalm 62:5 tells us to give our expectations over to God and wait upon Him.

Often a woman will say, "Well, he won't take over the spiritual leadership of the home, so someone has to." Have you tried praying and fasting over it? Have you stepped back and stopped taking things into **your** hands? If he leads a family devotional, do you make him feel like it was not good enough? Do you compare him to other men in the church? Do you build him up in the children's eyes, even if you do not always agree? It is better to disagree behind closed doors than to put down his authority in front of the children.

Remember, God gave your husband to you for your protection. Trust God to work on him and through him. God's timing is not ours, and He is still working on us also! Try suggesting in the form of a question instead of demanding. Ask, "What do you think about getting a new coat for Billy?" instead of, "You need to take Billy to the store and get him a new coat" or "Give me the money to get Billy a new coat." When you phrase your need in the form of a question, your husband will feel like you really value his opinion and want his advice in matters. Seek out his counsel. Let him make the decisions and lead your home.

Zipporah appeared to be rebellious, and the Bible says there is a price to pay for rebellion. First Samuel tells us "rebellion is as the sin of witchcraft." Do you want to be linked with the sin of witchcraft?

Carnal and Conniving

Another lesson we learn from Zipporah's life is not to be unequally yoked as stated in 2 Corinthians 6:14. This yoking can only bring sorrow and discord into the home. How can a man serve two masters? It is impossible. How can two walk together if they are not in agreement? They cannot! If you are already in this situation, though, the Bible gives hope (though it is not a promise) that the unbelieving husbands may be "won by the conversation (behavior) of the wives." *(1 Pet. 3:1)*

How are you doing? Have you neglected to follow one of the Lord's commands as Moses did? Are you living in rebellion to your husband? Or are you building him up and giving your expectations over to God instead of judging him and nagging him? Are you taking matters into your own hands, or are you seeking his advice and counsel? How about trusting God and allowing Him to work on your husband? Turn your frustrations over to the Lord and watch Him work a miracle in your marriage.

Zipporah's Roles

1. Shepherdess
2. Wife
3. Mother
4. Complainer

Zipporah's Character Traits

1. Ambition
2. Rebellion

Chapter 4

DELILAH

"The Lustful Woman"
"The Female Judas of the Old Testament"

Facts
Husband:	None known
Children:	None known
Occupation:	Harlot
Her name means:	"Languishing," "Lustful," "Delicate," "Dainty one"

Background

(Ex. 23:8; Josh. 13:3; Judg. 15:20; 16:4-5, 1 Tim. 6:10)

As ladies, we all have known one like her. By appearing helpless and dainty, she knew how to stroke a man's ego, dragging him down the pathway to destruction. Proverbs abounds with warnings about this very type of woman – the strange woman; the flatterer with her lips; the lady by the road beckoning the foolish, simple man. Samson was that man.

Samson, the twelfth judge of Israel, loved her. She lived in the valley of Sorek and was a foolish, deceptive, Philistine prostitute. She was hired by the Philistines to betray Samson for 1,100 pieces of silver. Who was this "languishing, delicate, dainty one?" Delilah!

Why did she resort to such a dastardly deed? Some say for money, some say for revenge against the Israelites, and yet others say it was pride – to look important to the VIP's. Whatever the reason, Delilah pocketed a large amount of money for her actions, far more than Judas did in betraying Jesus. If a silver shekel equaled $.75, she received $825 dollars from each ruler for her terrible deed. It appears there were five lords of the Philistines, bringing the grand total to $4,125!

The Enticement (Judg. 14:1-3, 15; 16:1-17; Prov. 5:3; 6:26; 7:26)

Samson's life was filled with conflict. One conflict led to another because he made poor decisions based upon the lust of the flesh. The first conflict began with his parents when, disrespecting their wishes and training, he became unequally yoked with a Philistine wife, demonstrating his rebellion.

Following this episode, he then faced conflict with his bride, leaving her to go fight with the Philistines. Upon his return home, she had been given to another. He then dealt with anger against his father-in-law and determined to get revenge.

As the days progressed, this mighty man of strength decided to take on the whole nation of the Philistines. However, by this time, the Philistines knew Samson's weakness--women. So, they connived with Delilah, formulating a plan of discovering this mighty man's strength.

Delilah seriously undertook the assignment. Samson began seeing her, and day after day she coaxed him to tell his source of strength. Her strategy seemed to be a "cat and mouse" game. "She pretended the greatest kindness even when she designed the greatest mischief..." *(Henry, Vol. II, p. 221)* On four different occasions, she begged him to tell the secret of his strength. Why didn't Samson suspect something after the first time? When we are backslidden, we have little if any spiritual discernment.

Notice the progression of her attack and his weakening. Delilah stroked his ego and flattered him, but he did not divulge the source of his strength. She then attacked his character and honesty. She continued to work on his honesty and finally cast doubt on his love for her and he finally gave in.

What a picture of the progression of sin in our lives – to flirt with sin, to think we are strong enough to go back again, to begin giving in, and then to cast all caution to the wind. Samson sowed carnality and reaped conflict. But he had a partner in his carnality – conniving Delilah.

The Fall   (Judg. 16:17-19; Jam. 4:7)

Delilah's persistence finally paid off. Perhaps she even used tears, a motivating trigger for the "delicate, helpless" one. Can't you just see Delilah dabbing at her eyes with a perfumed hankie, saying, "Samson, how can you say you love me *(sob),* when you won't share your secret with me?" *(sob)* Do we use tears to "get our own way?" Are we teaching our daughters to employ such a carnal technique? Shame on us!

Samson was physically strong, but morally weak. He could fight lions, but not his lust. Becoming a slave to passion, he forgot his consecration to God and allowed the Devil to "rock him to sleep." He "slept in the lap of lust and awakened in the hands of the Philistines." Two passions tormented him: gratifying Delilah or betraying himself. He was not spiritually strong enough to flee the evil as Joseph had.

> He could strangle a lion with his bare hands, but he could
> not strangle his lust for women. This free man of God
> willingly became slave to a harlot! How tragic that his
> close encounters with God's enemies did not lead him to
> a fervent relationship with his Lord. Samson's refusal to
> discipline himself physically coincided with his unwillingness
> to separate himself spiritually. *("Feature," Beyer, Dec. 27*[th]*)*

Delilah had no second thoughts about betraying him. Are you guilty of betraying others? Do you share confidences, making yourself look good, but causing the downfall of another's reputation? May it never be said of us that we have caused the downfall of another person!

Sad to say, Samson did not even realize he had lost his power with God. He thought he could flirt with temptation and rise above it. He shook himself as before, and "wist not that the Lord was departed from him." *(Judg. 16:20)*

Notice the first thing the Philistines did was to put Samson's eyes out, the source of his temptation and sin. He now was a slave. We do not see Delilah showing any sorrow or pity. She was heartless and did not even visit him in jail. After all, she had what she wanted—the money! She won again!

Nothing further is heard of Delilah in the Scriptures, yet her dastardly deed affected many, including herself. Perhaps she was in the crowd when Samson "brought the house down." Sin always yields death and destruction.

Conclusions (Deut. 7:3-4; Prov. 23:27; Eccl. 7:26; 2 Cor. 6:14)

Delilah used "personal charm for political ends." Like Bathsheba, she is remembered as a "woman who ruined a spiritual leader." She is a picture of the terrible evil a woman can accomplish by abusing and misusing her God-given gifts of charm. What a reminder to us! Are we training our daughters against this?

Samson's name was tarnished forever, and his people, the Israelites, shared in the suffering. Lust is powerful, and Satan plays for keeps. It takes away our common sense and decency, enslaving us. Hindering a normal, loving relationship, lust causes us to lose our fear of God, bringing "everlasting shame and contempt."

We need to beware that our strength does not become our weakness. Our spiritual enemies do not sleep when we sleep. Delilah lured Samson to sleep and then finished him off. Great exploits for God in the past do not guarantee present and future victories. We must stay vigilant and close to God!

We must take heed to God's Word and flee temptation and a deceitful lifestyle. Although we may not resort to harlotry, we may still become deceitful. Let us warn our sons and daughters to beware of the strange woman and encourage them to stay close to the Lord. We need to train our children to be honest, to flee temptation, and to be equally yoked with Christians of like faith.

Was the problem Samson's weakness or Delilah's wickedness? Both!

Delilah's Roles   Delilah's Character Traits

Delilah's Roles	Delilah's Character Traits
1. Harlot	1. Foolishness
2. Deceiver	2. Deceitfulness
3. Betrayer	3. Selfishness
4. Strange woman	4. Pride
5. Tormenter	5. Greediness
6. Phony	

Carnal and Conniving
Women of the Bible, volume 5

Notes:

Chapter 5

MICHAL
"The Unbelieving Wife"
"The Woman Whose Marriage Fell Apart"

Facts

Husband:	David and Phalti
Children:	None known
Occupation:	Princess, Homemaker
Her name means:	"Brook," "Who is like Jehovah?"

Background   (1 Sam. 14:49-50)

Michal (Mi' kuhl), the younger daughter of King Saul and Ahinoam was to become a king's wife. Blessed with three brothers and one sister, it appears she was the baby of the family. She lived the life of a princess in Saul's court, the first royal family in Israel. Perhaps she was accustomed to having the best of things, having every need met, and being spoiled and pampered. Although we find nothing about her mother's character, we know Saul was possessed with jealousy and obstinacy. His later life was consumed with killing David, the very man Michal would marry.

Michal fell in love with the giant slayer, David, and by a miraculous turn of events, became his first wife. Although she loved David, we will discover later in our study that she did not have the same love for the Lord that he did. Their unequal yoke was a situation ripe for disaster.

First Marriage (1 Sam. 16:12; 18:19-29)

Shortly after David's battle and victory over Goliath, Saul promised his oldest daughter, Merab, to David as wife. However, when the time came, Saul neglected to fulfill his promise and gave Merab to another. What an injustice to David! However, David never retaliated, but kept a right spirit of honor and respect toward Saul.

Noticing Michal's love for David, and being a conniving person himself, Saul determined to give the younger daughter to David. What young girl would not be impressed with David? He was handsome, strong, creative, and the hero of the day. Saul, being able to control Michal, wanted to "use" her against David because of his hatred and jealousy for David. Requiring no dowry except for a hundred foreskins of the Philistines, Saul thought his devious plan would work. Much to his surprise, David returned with double the amount!

When Saul realized his daughter's love, he feared David all the more. Why did Michal love David? For his good looks? For his fame and courage? We are not told the intent of her heart, but perhaps fascination and infatuation had overtaken her. They really had nothing in common. What a bad start they had to their relationship, with David's father-in-law hating him.

The Great Escape (1 Sam. 19:11-17)

Saul's hatred intensified so greatly that he sought to kill David. Demonstrating her loyalty and love to David, Michal informed him of the great danger to his life. She took initiative and courage, helping him to escape. However, we see her character flaws in this passage of Scripture:

1. **Deceit** – Michal tricked her father, allowing David more
      time to escape.   *(1 Sam. 19:13)*

2. **Idol worship** – She used an image, perhaps the cause of their later marital problems. *(1 Sam. 19:13, 16)*
3. **Lying** – She lied to protect herself. *(1 Sam. 19:14)*
4. **Misrepresentation of David** – She made her husband look like a murderer. *(1 Sam. 19:17)*

God could and would have handled all of these areas!

Her Second Marriage (1 Sam. 20:1; 22:1; 23:16; 25:44; 2 Sam. 3:13)

Things progressed from bad to worse in the marriage. With David gone, Saul had opportunity to control Michal's affairs. Why didn't Michal seek David or go after him? Or did she even have opportunity? Saul gave Michal to Phalti, probably to spite David. We are not told if she loved Phalti or if she was willing or unwilling. Was she tired of waiting on David?

It appears the separation covered a long period of time, as 2 Samuel 3:1 states, "there was long war between the house of Saul and the house of David." David took other wives during this time who blessed him with six sons. However, it seems he had not forgotten Michal, and perhaps his heart still yearned for his first love. When asked to make a league with Abner for the kingdom, David requested the restoration of his wife, Michal.

Restoration (2 Sam. 3:13-16)

Dispatching messengers to Saul's son Ishbosheth, David demanded the return of Michal. Imagine how Phalti felt after years of marriage to her! Michal was taken from him, and Scripture reveals his broken heart, as he followed behind her crying. Abner rudely ordered him to return to his home.

Throughout this episode, we are given no insight on Michal's reaction. Was she upset? Had her love for David waned? Did she look forward to the glory of being a king's wife?

After no communication for years, how would this marriage work out?

Change of Heart   (2 Sam. 6:16-22)

Many events transpired in David's life following Michal's return. His coronation took place in Hebron; Jerusalem became the capital; the king of Tyre built David a palace; and David took on yet more wives and concubines. Continuing as a military leader, David's fame grew and spread. Now it was time to bring the ark of God to Jerusalem for a permanent home.

In all of his zeal and excitement, "David danced before the Lord with all his might." *(2 Sam. 6:14)* We now see Michal's true spiritual condition. Scripture tells us she despised David in her heart. This is recorded twice, in 2 Samuel 6:16 and in 1 Chronicles 15:29. She did not seem to share David's religious fervor or understand it. Notice that she was not even with him at this high point in his life, but was home watching out a window. Perhaps she did not like mingling with the common people. She was more Saul's daughter than David's wife. The Scripture confirms this in 2 Samuel 6:20 and 1 Chronicles 15:29, calling her, "Michal, the daughter of Saul."

> Although she had loved him, risked her life for his safety,
> she now abhors him for his loss of royal dignity. Her
> haughtiness was shocked by David's participation in such
> an excitable demonstration.   *(Lockyer, p. 110)*

Theirs was probably a mixed marriage, with Michal perhaps the unbeliever. She may have loved David, but not his God. Remember the idols in the beginning of our study?

David returned to bless his household, only to find a cold, nagging, unbelieving wife. Michal became bitter, resentful, and sarcastic. She had the same problem as Miriam and Zipporah and was unable to control her emotions. Matthew Henry says, "She scorned him at a distance and scolded him when he came home!"

Carnal and Conniving
Women of the Bible, volume 5

(Henry, Vol. II, p. 477) May that never be said of us concerning our husbands!

Michal turned David's worship into something lewd and base as a cover-up for her own unbelief. She was "passing the buck," blaming David for her unbelief. This is the second time she misrepresented him! Alexander Whyte states, "Michal is a divine looking-glass for all angry and outspoken wives." What a tragic turn of events! At the highest point of David's career, she was not there for him!

Haven't you seen it happen, ladies? A lady prays and prays for her husband to get saved! That unbelieving husband finally gives his heart to the Lord. The holy wife then criticizes him for not doing things perfectly, for working too much at the church, for not getting baptized soon enough, for not having family devotions, for not going soul-winning, and on and on. Her expectations are so high; no one could meet them. She is not there for him at the high point of his life. They finally each become discouraged and quit going to church altogether.

What is wrong with us, ladies? We need to come alongside and be the encourager and helpmeet we were intended to be. We only need make our husbands happy, and let God make them holy. Besides, He can do a much better job than we can!! Are you hindering you spouse? Are you "trashing or treasuring" your marital relationship?

> Cruel jokes about a spouse's personality, taking lightly a
> sacrifice made, making fun of a deficiency, mocking a love
> for God – these are all ways a woman might trash a relation-
> ship which God intends for her to treasure. . .
> *(Handford, Women Under the Kings, p. 17)*

David took his stand for the Lord, informing Michal that God had chosen him as a ruler, and he **would worship Him.** Michal's sharp tongue and jealous heart helped ruin her marriage. She refused the instruction of Proverbs 21:23: "Whoso keepeth his mouth and his tongue keepeth his soul from troubles."

Conclusions

(1 Sam. 18:19; 2 Sam. 6:23; 21:8-9; 1 Chr. 16:22; Prov. 12:13; Amos 3:3; Matt 7:1; 1 Cor. 3:11; 2 Cor. 6:14; Eph 4:26)

What grievous judgment fell upon Michal! Second Samuel 6:23 states, **"Therefore,** Michal the daughter of Saul had no child unto the day of her death." God shows us the tragic consequences of speaking out against His anointed. As you recall, barrenness was a great shame, and Michal would go through her life bearing the mark of her sin.

We never hear of her asking David for forgiveness. Her early love for David was not enough to sustain their relationship, showing us the tragedy of an unequal yoke.

Although Michal bore no children of her own, she raised her sister's five sons, only later to see them hanged as a result of more judgment upon Saul's house.

Her life was full of tragedy. Her father had an evil spirit and committed suicide. She was torn from two husbands, and her five nephews were hanged. What a sad and lonely life! If she would only have opened her heart to David's God, she could have experienced the comfort that only He can give!

What lessons can we learn from this lady's life? The most important one is basing our foundation upon Christ. Michal never had that foundation. She and David could not walk together because they were unequally yoked. Marrying for good looks or fame is not the basis for a prosperous, strong marriage.

Another lesson is the importance of bridling our tongues. Michal's outspokenness and sharp tongue revealed her heart's condition and caused God's judgment to fall upon her. Because she judged God's man and spoke out against him, she paid a heavy price. How unwise it is to speak out against God's man, a lesson reiterated time and again in the Scriptures. Good examples are Miriam and Zipporah. The Scriptures teach, "Touch not mine anointed, and do my prophets no harm." *(Psalm 105:15)* Ladies, we need to bridle our tongues among our friends, being careful not to speak against our husbands, our pastors, or those in leadership.

A third lesson is the necessity of seeking forgiveness early in our relationships, not allowing problems to fester and turn into bitterness. Pride keeps us from asking forgiveness. Often we expect our husbands to read our minds and know why we are upset. Why not quietly and calmly share your heart? Perhaps you are not the only offended one!

Dear lady, are you facing marriage problems and turmoil? Turn your expectations over to God, bridle your tongue, and forgive. Keep your marriage built upon the foundation of Jesus Christ, and beware of a "Michal spirit," beginning with dreams of happiness and ending with bitterness and decay.

> . . .First we see a young, beautiful, loving, courageous girl.
> But at the end we see a disillusioned, bickering woman with
> an inner poverty of spirit, one oppressed with many tragedies.
> *(Deen, "All of the Women," p. 100)*

Michal's Roles

1. Princess
2. Wife
3. Unbeliever
4. Aunt
5. Foster mother

Michal's Character Traits

1. Courage
2. Deceitfulness
3. Bitterness
4. Outspokenness
5. Jealousy
7. Sarcasm
8. Scorn
9. Pride

Carnal and Conniving
Women of the Bible, volume 5

Notes:

Chapter 6

JEZEBEL

"A Cursed Woman"
"The Feminist"
"The Woman Who Was a She-Devil"

Facts

Husband:	Ahab
Children:	Ahaziah, Jehoram, Athaliah
Occupation:	Queen
Her name means:	"Chaste," "Free from carnal connection," "Unmarried"

Background   (1 Kings 11:1; 16:30-33)

What do you think of when you hear the name "Jezebel?" Do you know anyone bearing that name? Would you name your daughter after her? Where did she come from?

Sidon was a port city located on the Mediterranean, known for "artistic metal work, purple dyeing, and glass blowing." *(Pictorial Bible Dictionary, p. 792)* The Sidonians were obsessed with an ardent love for Baal and caught up with materialism. The inhabitants were largely Greek, and later, the city was "noted for its school of philosophy under Augustus and Tiberius." *(International Standard Bible Encyclopedia, p. 2786)* The city is often linked in Scripture with Tyre and was visited by Christ and Paul.

The Israelites failed to conquer this city, and it was always to be a thorn in their side. Jezebel, perhaps the most godless and wicked woman we will study, came from this port city. She was the daughter of Ethbaal, King of the Zidonians. Like other inhabitants of Sidon, she was entrenched with Baal worship, known for its child sacrifices and attempted control of weather and fertility. Materialism also pervaded her life, and she determined to have it all, no matter what the cost.

Jezebel married Ahab, the King of Israel and introduced Baal worship to the Israelites. Ahab sinned by marrying her, and she apparently influenced him in his own worship, as 1 Kings 16:32-33 tells us that Ahab made an altar for Baal and a grove, provoking God more than any of the former kings.

Persecutor of the Prophets (1 Kings 18:4, 13, 19; 19:1-3)

Jezebel was the first female religious persecutor, threatening and killing men of God. Being completely entrenched in idolatry, she entertained the prophets of Baal right at her own dinner table. What a hospitable queen she was! First Kings 18:19 totals these prophets at 850! What a huge dinner party!

The godly prophet, Elijah, was the only man to stand up to her. Her own husband, Ahab, could not even control her, letting her have her own way most of the time. When she could not get her way, she just did away with the people involved.

Elijah experienced great victory at Mt. Carmel when 450 prophets of Baal were slain. In a fit of hatred and rage, Jezebel threatened Elijah and swore out a warrant for his arrest and death. Perhaps Ahab tried to stir her up, telling her only what Elijah had done and giving no credit to God for the events at Mt. Carmel. Fear overtook Elijah, and he fled the scene!

Liar and Murderess (Num. 36:7; Ezek. 46:18; 1 Kings 21:1-16)

Ahab coveted his neighbor Naboth's vineyard, but Naboth would not give it to him, due to inheritance rights. Ahab pouted, went to bed, and would not eat. He was a weak and spineless man. Jezebel showed disrespect for him and became sarcastic saying, "Do you govern the Kingdom of Israel or not? Get up, eat, and be merry. I will get the vineyard for you!" She took matters into her own hands and determined to get it herself. Notice her pride and usurpation of authority! She was a bully!

Becoming a liar, she wrote letters in Ahab's name. She used religious purposes to cover up her foul deed by proclaiming a fast, by making the king seem as important as God, and by setting up false witnesses against Naboth. She twisted the law to fit her purposes. What a devilish and wicked woman she was!

Consider her power! None of the men in the city would stand up to her. The plan worked, and Naboth was stoned, making Jezebel a murderess and Ahab an accomplice. What a wicked, evil plot over a parcel of earth!

Prophecy of Her Death   (1 Kings 21:17, 21-24, 27-29)

The Spirit of the Lord dealt with Elijah, forcing him to take action. He approached Ahab and pronounced the whole family's doom. Notice again the principle: we are never the only ones affected by our sin! He prophesied Jezebel's death would occur, and that she would be eaten by dogs!

Ahab, knowing what was right to do, demonstrated humility by repenting and fasting. God withheld the doom for several years and rewarded Ahab's "external services" with "external mercies." *(Matthew Henry, Vol. II, p. 699)* However, although Ahab confessed, he did not share anything with Jezebel about the situation. We see no reaction from her.

Influential Wife and Mother   (1 Kings 21:25-26; 22:51-53; 2 Kings 3:1-3; 9:22; 11:1)

Scripture reiterates the power of influence a woman wields in her home and family. Again, we are told that there was never a king like Ahab who sold himself to work wickedness. Why? His wife stirred him up! She was a great helpmeet in the area of evil. How about you, dear friend? Do you incite your husband, manipulating him to make bad decisions? Or do you stir him up to good works?

She not only influenced her husband, but also warped her children's character. Ahaziah reigned two years in Israel, served and worshipped Baal, and provoked God to anger just as his father had done. Jehoram reigned twelve years and "wrought evil," although he did put away the image of Baal. Athaliah, like her mother Jezebel, carried Baal worship into Judah. All of Jezebel's children followed in her evil footsteps, as contrasted to Jochebed whose children all served God! Jezebel and Athaliah were missionaries for the Devil, ensnaring Israel and Judah in the worship of Baal.

Jezebel's sinful life was about to catch up with her. She had sowed to the wind and was about to reap the whirlwind.

Prophecy Fulfilled   (1 Kings 22:37-38; 2 Kings 1:2, 17; 9:7, 10, 22-26; 9:30-37; 10:1, 7-8)

God's hand was stayed only so long! Elijah's prophecy would be fulfilled! King Ahab died in battle with the Syrians, and the dogs licked up his blood. The oldest son, Ahaziah, died after falling out of a window.

Elisha anointed Jehu king and instructed him to finish off Ahab's family. Jehoram, the younger son, died after Jehu shot him with an arrow. Athaliah would die while trying to commit treason!

Filled with pomp and pride, Jezebel "dolled herself up" either to thwart Jehu or to die in pride. Perhaps she thought her use of intimidation would prevail once again!   We do not see her grieving over any of her losses. She was taken up only with herself. Although she was in humbling circumstances, she refused to humble herself and admit the hand of God in her son's death. What a hardened heart she possessed!

Her own servants disrespected her and threw her out the window where she was trampled upon by Jehu's horses. Jehu thought she should have a proper burial since she was a king's daughter; however, he found nothing but her skull, her feet, and her hands. Prophecy was fulfilled to a "t." The dogs ate her flesh, and her body became as dung. She truly was a "cursed woman!" The whole Ahab household was destroyed, including Ahab's seventy sons whose heads were cut off, put in baskets, and delivered to Jezreel.

Proverbs 6:16-19 describes Jezebel perfectly, instructing us in the things God hates:

> These six things doth the Lord hate: yea seven are an
> abomination unto him: A proud look, a lying tongue,
> and hands that shed innocent blood, An heart that
> deviseth wicked imaginations, feet that be swift in
> running to mischief, A false witness that speaketh lies,
> and he that soweth discord among brethren.

Conclusions   (Prov. 10:7; 22:1; Eccl. 7:1; Rev. 2:20)

Jezebel harmfully used her power of influence. This influence reached nationwide. She is a perfect example of what a woman **should not be:** domineering, aggressive, strong-willed, stubborn, conniving, cruel, and ruthless. She would stop at nothing to get her own way, because she had no fear of God. She looms as a beacon to warn us to submit our will to that of our heavenly Father's.

Pride and rebellion filled her life to the very end, with no death-bed conversion for her! Demonstrating a feminist spirit, she masterminded Ahab's wickedness, misusing her talents and gifts of intelligence. She did more to hurt Israel than all of Solomon's wives! Throughout the Scriptures, her name is **always** associated with evil and wickedness.

How can we apply lessons learned from her life to ours? First, we learn it is never wise to usurp authority or take family matters into our own hands. There may be times when we do not like a decision our husband has made. We need to take it to the Lord, realizing if we sow to the wind, we will reap the whirlwind, like Jezebel did.

Our actions are important, as our children are watching, and they learn very quickly! If our daughters see us "stirring up" Daddy or disrespecting him, they will copy the same pattern with their own husbands someday.

To promote her own evil deeds, Jezebel called a day of fasting. May our families never see us use "religious purposes" to cover up "foul deeds."

Revelation 2:20 likewise shows us how Jezebel's name lives on in God's warning to the church of Thyatira against the doctrines of Baalism and Nicolaitanism. They had allowed a so-called prophetess to seduce them into committing fornication and eating things sacrificed to idols! Jezebel would never live down the wicked reputation she had built.

Jezebel is proof that pride always goes before a fall. She was "contaminated by the world, conformed to the world, and ultimately condemned with the world." *(Wiersbe, p. 52)* Beware, stay on guard, keep your weapon (God's Word) handy – don't let the world contaminate you!!

Jezebel's Roles

1. Wife
2. Mother
3. Queen
4. Usurper
5. Liar
6. Murderess
7. Persecutor

Jezebel's Character Traits

1. Aggressiveness
2. Deceitfulness
3. Stubbornness
4. Pride
5. Ambition
6. Rebellion
7. Ruthlessness
8. Domination

Chapter 7

ATHALIAH
"That Wicked Woman"

Facts

Husband:	Jehoram
Children:	Ahaziah, Jehosheba
	Other unnamed sons
Occupation:	Queen
Her name means:	"Taken away from the Lord,"
	"Jehovah has afflicted"

Background
(2 Kings 8:16-18, 26-27; 2 Chr. 21:4-6; 24:7)

Athaliah followed in the footsteps of her mother, Jezebel, in many ways. Like her mother, she married a king, Jehoram, the king of Judah—another mixed marriage! Jehoram had come from a godly family, with Jehoshaphat as his father. Imagine his father and mother's dismay at the unequal yoke! Henry says, "Those that are ill-matched are already half-ruined." (*Matthew Henry, Vol. II, p. 752)* The handwriting was on the wall for Jehoram.

One would assume that Athaliah had learned her lesson from witnessing the demise and destruction of her own parents, but this was not the case! She continued to sow idolatry throughout Judah.

Although she was a wife and mother of several sons, being a helpmeet and homemaker were not fulfilling to this wicked woman. She pursued an agenda of her own, seeking political prestige and power, just as Jezebel had done.

Imitating Jezebel's influence and lacking a servant's heart, nothing could prevent Athaliah from getting what she wanted. She was a "chip off the old block," and would not be hindered in her political and materialistic goals! She was a power-hungry woman who cared little what she had to do to attain it!

Determined to spread Baal worship, and patterning herself after her godless mother, Athaliah even counseled her own sons to spread wickedness. We are led to believe that she also stirred up her husband, due to the wording in 2 Chronicles 21:6: ". . .for he had the daughter of Ahab to wife: and he wrought that which was evil in the eyes of the Lord."

The Quest for Power   (2 Kings 11:1-4; 2 Chr. 21:6, 22: 2-4, 10)

Jehoram died, and Ahaziah, his son occupied the throne, beginning his reign at the age of 42. He continued the evil reign for one year. Scripture tells us his own mother counseled him to do wickedly. *(2 Chr. 22:3)* What a sad commentary on Athaliah as a mother! May it never be said of us that we have counseled our children to do wickedness! However, if they see us caving in to carnal and fleshly appetites, they may follow suit. It seems the whole royal family was consumed with the wicked lifestyle. Ahaziah's own family members, the house of Ahab, "were his counselors after the death of his father to his destruction."*(2 Chr. 22:4)*

Following Ahaziah's short reign, Athaliah's hunger for power became so great that she destroyed all the royal seed! What possessed this woman to kill her own family? She was a carnal, cruel, conniving woman with no conscience. Satan used her in an attempt to destroy the line of Christ.

Why did she destroy them? Matthew Henry gives two thoughts:

1. She had a **"spirit of revenge"** and anger at God to destroy the house of David. *(Henry, Vol. II, p. 766)*

44

2. She had a **"spirit of ambition"** for power directed in the
wrong manner . Her thirst for rule consumed her,
and she would tolerate no competition.

God help us as mothers not to feel like we are in competition
with our own children and grandchildren! What happened to
Athaliah's maternal instinct? How could a woman stoop to such
a dastardly deed? She killed her own grandchildren, and
possibly some of her own sons!

The Divine Intervention   (2 Chr. 22:11-12; 23:1-3; 24:4; Psa. 27:5)

However, no one can thwart God's will, and a 911 team
appeared on the scene, in the form of a preacher and his wife.
"God will raise up protectors for those whom He will have
protected." *(Henry, Vol. II, p. 766)* Jehosheba, an unnoticed
lady and a preacher's wife, kept the Davidic line of Christ intact.
She rescued Joash, the grandson of Athaliah, and hid him. Was
Jehosheba Athaliah's own daughter?   Scripture is not clear,
although we are told in 2 Chronicles 22:11 that she was the
daughter of the king.   How did her parents feel about her
marrying a preacher?   If she had come from the wicked royal
family, it proves that we do not have to allow a bad past or
wicked environment to ruin our present lives! God is powerful!
Joash was a "brand plucked out of the fire." God provided
for him and protected him! Where did Jehosheba hide the little
fellow? She hid him in the temple – a place where no one would
look, as Athaliah would seldom be found there. (Note: Joash
would later repair the house of the Lord when he became king.)
Athaliah knew nothing of the matter and reigned for six years
over the land. The power behind the throne had finally become
the power on the throne! Hers was a reign of tyranny, preparing
the people's hearts for a drastic change. Little did she know the
consequences of her sin were about to be her demise.

After six years, Jehoida, Jehosheba's husband, fetched the rulers, captains, and guards and let them know the secret, swearing them to secrecy. There was a king!

The Powerful Plan (2 Kings 11:5-10; 2 Chr. 23:4-10)

God's man devised a plan. One-third of the men were to keep watch over the king's house, one-third were to watch the gate of Sur and the back gate, and one-third were to watch the house of the Lord where the king was. Joash had his own personal bodyguard with weapons.

The people respected and loved Jehoida. They obeyed and explicitly followed his plan. They probably hated Athaliah. If you recall, Jezebel's own servants threw her out the window to her death. Jehoida gave them David's spears and shield from the temple. Everybody took their places! Would the plan work?

The Surprise Coronation (Ex. 25:16; 31:18; 2 Kings 11:12; 2 Chr. 23:11)

The coronation ceremony began! Joash is estimated to have been about seven to eight years of age, one of the youngest kings on record.

Four major things took place during the big event. They crowned him, showing kingly power. They gave him the testimony – the Law – showing the Word of God would be his rule. They anointed him, demonstrating the Spirit's approval of him for service. They clapped their hands, signifying their approval, acceptance, and subjection to their new king. What a day of celebration it was! It had been a long time since the people had experienced a godly ruler! They were more than ready!

The Sudden Death   (2 Kings 11:13-16, 20; 2 Chr. 23:12-15, 21; Prov. 11:10)

Athaliah heard the noise and wondered what was going on! After all, she had not planned any party. For once she was in a hurry to get to the house of God. What will it take to get us to the house of God on a regular basis? A tragedy? Like Jezebel, we see her hastening to her own destruction. Her own servants withheld their loyalty to reveal what was happening!

She went along to the temple. Imagine the look of surprise on her face when she saw a new king! Overcome with anger, she tore her clothing and cried, "Treason! Treason!" She was no longer heir to the throne! Her quest for power now became a quest for protection.

Realizing her own life was in jeopardy, she fled the scene. The priest sent the captains after her to kill her. However, they were not to desecrate the temple by killing her there, and they were to kill anyone who followed her.

She pursued a horse path and was killed there. What joy among the people as her six-year reign of terror was over! Notice she was left in a horse path to be trampled upon just as Jezebel had been left to the dogs. Finally, there was peace in the city! What rejoicing and celebration took place!

Conclusions

Second Chronicles 24:7 calls Athaliah "that wicked woman." She depicts a woman with no morals, no conscience, and no fear of God. We see the sowing and reaping principle operating time after time throughout the whole story of Athaliah. She was a woman hungry for power—a murderess, a feminist! She was the only woman to rule over Judah and possessed absolutely no heart of compassion for the job. Lacking a conscience and possessing a hardened heart, she would have killed even her own grandson.

Carnal and Conniving
Women of the Bible, volume 5

She used her power of influence in a very injurious manner, thinking to solidify her reign for years to come.

> Her very name is an execration. She put the whole nation under the shadow of a great horror. She trampled on all faith. She violated all obligation. She lived with the shrieks of those she butchered in her ears. She lived with her hands red with the blood of princes and princesses. She died, frantic with rage, with the accusation of Treason on her lips. She died in the barnyard under the battleaxes of an aroused people.
>
> *(Lockyer, "All the Women, p. 33)*

However, God's purpose is never thwarted! He always comes on the scene at just the right time! He wants to come on the scene for you—first of all to save your soul, then to give you victorious, abundant Christian living!

Through Athaliah's life, we follow the path of pride, seeing her fall and destruction. Wicked people only prosper for a season, and there **is** a price to pay. Her life teaches us that a thirst for power can cause one's loss of morals or common sense. Moreover, we need to work **with** our husbands, not **against** or **above** them.

There are many similarities between Jezebel and Athaliah:

1. Both married kings.
2. Both had mixed marriages.
3. Both were hungry for power and had a feminist spirit.
4. Both were wicked and cruel.
5. Both spread Baal worship.
6. Both counseled their sons to do wickedly.
7. Both hastened their own deaths.
8. Both had disloyal servants.
9. Both were murderesses.

What a challenge Athaliah's life is to us as mothers and wives of today! May we share positive, God-fearing traits with our daughters! May we use the Word of God to train and guide them! May our love and respect for our husbands be shown through an everyday, ongoing submission. May we beg God for a humble heart and spirit to serve our families! May a "Jezebel or Athaliah spirit" never be connected with our names!!

Athaliah's Roles   Athaliah's Character Traits

1. Wife
2. Mother
3. Queen
4. Usurper
5. Dictator
6. Murderess
7. Idolatress
8. Persecutor

1. Determination
2. Cruelty
3. Envy
4. Pride
5. Greed
6. Rebellion
7. Ruthlessness
8. Domination

Notes:

Chapter 8

HERODIAS
&
SALOME

"The Jezebel and Athaliah of the New Testament"

Facts

Herodias

Husband:	Philip, Herod Antipas
Children:	Salome
Occupation:	Queen
Her name means:	"Heroic," "Seed of a hero"

Salome

Husband:	Philip the tetrarch
	Aristobulus, king of Chalcis
Children:	Unknown
Occupation:	Princess
Her name means:	"Peace," "Very shady"

Background   (Matt. 2:1, 3, 12, 22; Luke 13:32)

Our story opens in the king's palace where Herod the tetrarch of Galilee ruled. This royal family was one filled with lust, incest, greed, vengeance, and debauchery. Hunger for power and cruelty filled their days of reign. Lacking a fear of God, their lives were a continual decline of apostasy, murder, and deceit. Great attempts of murder were made against the prophets and men of God in their lives, including against the Lord Jesus.

Herodias was the daughter of Aristobulus, the son of Herod the Great who had earnestly sought to kill Christ when He was a baby. Her mother's name was Mariamne, and she was an Edomite.

Herodias' first marriage was to Philip, Herod's brother, meaning she married her uncle. From this union came their daughter Salome. Like Jezebel, Herodias had a quest for wealth, power, and prestige and determined to get it no matter what.

As our story begins, she now has a new husband, Herod Antipas, also the son of Herod the Great. Herod had divorced his first wife and taken her. Jesus calls this same Herod a "fox" in Luke 13:32.

The Quarrel and Quest (Prov. 28:23; Matt. 14:4-6; Mark 6:15-21; Luke 3:19-20)

John the Baptist, the forerunner of Christ, had rebuked Herod for his sin of adultery and incest, saying, "It is not lawful for thee to have her." *(Matt. 14:4b)* John, filled with boldness, stood up to the "leader of the day." Henry says, "Those ministers that would be found faithful in the work of God, must not be afraid of the face of man."

Herodias was so full of anger that she wanted him killed. *(Mark 6:19)* Her position and power were threatened. Would Herod listen too closely to John's advice? Would she lose her prestigious position? Wielding her power of influence, she persuaded Herod to throw John into jail. How do we know that? Because Matthew 14:3 and Mark 6:17 tell us Herod acted for "Herodias' sake." Because of his fear and his wife's rage, Herod imprisoned the preacher. Scholars estimate that John had been imprisoned for a year and a half. Why didn't Herod just go ahead and kill John?

Carnal and Conniving
Women of the Bible, volume 5

1. He feared the multitude (**not God**). They liked John.
2. He knew John was a prophet.
3. He feared John.
   a. He knew John was just.
   b. He knew John was holy. (John had kept his testimony in prison.)
   c. He liked John's preaching and heard him gladly!

Herod had watched John and had seen him do many things! Had Herodias kept Herod from turning to God? What a power we as ladies have! We can encourage our husbands, friends, and children to grow in spiritual things, or we can be discontent like Herodias and actually turn them in the other direction.

Sad to say, Herod was like many people who sit in our churches today. He respected John until John put his finger on Herod's sin. Herodias was not about to be thwarted. She bided her time and awaited her chance. The Bible uses the words, "but when," and "when a convenient day was come." We see bitterness and hard-heartedness pervade her whole being. Like Jezebel, she determined not to respond to the man of God or the Word of God.

Dear ladies, may it never be said of us! May our hearts ever be soft and our wills pliable to God's will for our lives! May we allow the Word of God to permeate our hearts through the working of the Holy Spirit. May we never give in to bitterness and hard-heartedness like Herodias did.

The Birthday Party
(Prov. 6:2; 23:31-33; Eccl. 5:6; Matt. 14:6; Mk. 6:21-23)

The occasion finally presented itself—Herod's birthday! Weaving a wicked web of deceit and carnality, Herodias contrived a method for her madness! Perhaps she even planned the whole party, including the guest list. All the "bigwigs" and

VIP's were invited—the lords, the captains, and the chiefs of state.

What better idea than to use her own daughter to provide the entertainment? Salome willingly followed along with the plan, dancing sensuously before all the men, stirring their passions! What kind of mother would condone and even promote such a thing? Only an ungodly, vengeful, power-driven woman! Through this Biblical account, we see the results of dancing. Nowhere in the Bible do we see mixed dancing. Dancing was usually done for amusement and ended in destruction, except for the time David danced before the Lord in praise.

We do not see Salome hesitating or questioning the diabolical plan. Was she aware of the consequences?

What a wicked, vile example Herodias was to her daughter! "Herodias was willing to sacrifice her child's modesty in order to bend Herod to her will." *(Lockyer, All the Women, p. 68-69)* She was a true "Jezebel" in every sense of the word." What similarities did the two possess?

1. Both sought to kill preachers. (Elijah, John the Baptist)
2. Both possessed the same character traits. (rebellion, lack of submission, desire for power and control)
3. Both taught their children cruelty.
4. Both of their husbands sinned when they married them.

Salome followed through with the entertainment. The dance stirred the senses of Herod and his guests. In fact, Herod was so pleased after the dance that he vowed to give Salome anything she asked for up to the half of his kingdom. Matthew Henry speculates that perhaps Herod was part of the plot himself and knew what was going to be asked!

The Request and Revenge <small>(Matt. 14:8; Mk. 6:24-25)</small>

After Herod's offer, we see Salome asking her mother what to do. Herodias instructed her to ask for the head of John the Baptist.

Note their mother-daughter relationship:

1. Herodias had total influence over Salome.
2. The girl had apparently picked up her mother's offense.
3. She probably had the same attitude toward John.

Be careful, moms! Do we criticize the men of God who are trying to influence our children's lives? Scripture says we are to honor them and touch not God's anointed. Gather your children around you, and take time to pray for their leaders instead of criticizing them. Our children will pick up our attitudes and offenses.

Salome does not flinch, does not appear shocked or disgusted, and proceeds to follow through with the bizarre request. Notice that she even asked more than her mother had instructed. She asked for the head to be given to her on a charger, like a dish of meat at a feast!

The Dastardly Deed <small>(Matt. 14:9-11; Mk. 6:26-28; Jam. 1:14)</small>

Herod was exceedingly sorry, but now he had to "save face." He was not about to be publicly humiliated. Would his wicked oath justify a wicked deed? Herod was not man enough nor honorable enough to make the oath void. Who does this remind us of? Pilate! Herod had made a rash oath, and all those present knew it! However, he was only sorry. His favor with the people was more important to him than his conscience. His deed would not work sorrow to repentance. He just walked around with a guilty conscience! Henry notes that "many a man sins with regret that never has regret for his sin." *(Henry, Vol. V, p. 199)*

Carnal and Conniving

Herod was a pawn in his wife's hands. "As Jezebel had made a tool of Ahab to slay the prophets of Jehovah, so Herodias had made a tool of Herod Antipas to behead John the Baptist." *(Deen, All the Women, p. 187)* Herod killed the very man he had respected and heard gladly. This same Herod would later persecute Jesus, mocking Him and arraying Him in a purple robe. *(Luke 23:11)*

> Do not let anyone cast a spell over you. I pray you, escape
> for your life; run for it when vice hunts you. . .it is supremely
> dangerous to be under the fascination of a wicked woman or
> a vicious man. God help you to rise above it by His Spirit,
> for if you are hearers of the word and doers of evil, you will
> end in being Herods, and nothing more.   *(Spurgeon, p. 494)*

The execution immediately took place, and Salome delivered the head to her mother on a platter! What kind of women were these? One historian even records Herodias pricking John's tongue with a needle! What wicked, vile, and blood-thirsty women! Abraham Kuyper describes such women:

> When she chooses to do good, she blesses more than ever a
> man can. But the moment she surrenders to sin, her hatred
> toward the men of God is much more passionate, much
> fiercer, much more fatal.   *(Kuyper, p. 58)*

He likens the event to Eve conspiring with Satan to persuade her husband to oppose God.

Ladies, we need to beware! Our churches, homes, and schools are filled with bitter, hard-hearted women – women who seek revenge, power and prestige—women who will stop at nothing to attain it! May our hearts and lives be Spirit-controlled! May our lives be spent in service to our Lord and Master, not bent on climbing a ladder of success, trampling everyone on our way. May any root of bitterness be cut out at its root before it defiles many. *(Heb. 12:15)*

Conclusions

We learn many practical applications from the lives of Herodias and Salome. Once again, we see the power of influence we have on others. Our attitudes are important! Children, husbands, and friends are watching!

Herodias refused to respond to God's Word in her life. Our children watch to see if we respond to the preaching and teaching of the Word of God. Is our life secular throughout the week and sacred only on Sunday? Or do we allow the Word of God to permeate and influence every decision we make every day? How long has it been since you have responded during an altar call at your church? Do you allow your heart to be touched and convicted by the Holy Spirit? Do you have a personal, daily walk with the Lord Jesus Christ? **Our families are watching!**

Another practical application from this Biblical account is to beware of using your children to your own advantage. Your children are not puppets to manipulate or to cover up your bad deeds. You dare not use them to accomplish your will.

Although Herodias had everything a woman could want materially, she languished spiritually. The things of this world will pass away. We can take nothing but our families with us. Oh, that we might be godly ladies, not always looking to material blessings!

Historian Josephus tells us that Herodias met her fate. She tried to convince her husband to demand the title of king from the emperor. The request was refused, and Herod was exiled. Their days of reign ended in shame. The only positive note about Herodias is that she remained true to Herod. Although she was offered freedom, it is said she refused. Both she and Herod died in Gaul. "Her ambition became her downfall." *(Josephus)*

Salome is a picture to us of blind obedience, although she was old enough to know better. Perhaps she had totally incorporated her mother's wicked values, as she displayed no hesitance in the dastardly scheme.

Carnal and Conniving
Women of the Bible, volume 5

Tradition holds that while Salome was walking over ice in the winter, "the ice broke, and she slipt in up to her neck which was cut through by the sharpness of the ice." *(Henry, Vol. V, p. 201)* Did God require her head for John the Baptist's?

May the lessons from Herodias and Salome motivate us to search our own hearts, to dig out any root of bitterness, to flee vile and vicious influences, to keep our hands and tongues off God's men, and to keep our hearts in tune with God and His precious Word.

Herodias' Roles

1. Wife
2. Mother
3. Adulteress
4. Accomplice
5. Schemer
6. Murderess

Herodias' Character Traits

1. Determination
2. Cruelty
3. Envy
4. Pride
5. Greed
6. Rebellion
7. Ruthlessness
8. Ambition

Salome's Roles

1. Dancer
2. Princess
3 Persecutor
4. Accomplice
5. Schemer
6. Murderess
7. Idolatress
8. Temptress

Salome's Character Traits

1. Determination
2. Cruelty
3. Envy
4. Pride
5. Greed
6. Rebellion
7. Ruthlessness
8. Ambition

Chapter 9

SAPPHIRA
"The Woman Who Dropped Dead"

Facts	
Husband:	Ananias
Children:	Unknown
Occupation:	Housewife
Her name means:	"Sapphire," "Beautiful," "Pleasant"

Background

They lived in Jerusalem and were both faithful "church-goers." Perhaps they had even been part of the early prayer meeting and the planting of the first church. Surely they had heard Peter preach and witnessed the power of Pentecost. To their amazement, three thousand souls were saved! Were they a part of that number or just curious onlookers? Then the miracles began with a lame man found "walking, and leaping, and praising God." They wanted to be a part of this new movement!

Their names? Ananias and Sapphira. Although her name meant "sapphire," "the only sparkle she was able to give us was that of a grim warning." *(Karssen, Vol. II, p. 216)* They were soon to become living (or should we say *dead?*) proof of the Scripture in Numbers 32:23: ". . . and be sure your sin will find you out." Although they were a part of the early church and great revival, they had an internal heart problem which was about to manifest itself in their actions – that of greed and deceit! Like Achan in the Old Testament, they thought it was possible to hide or cover their sin.

Just as Satan tried to destroy all of Creation with the first couple, Adam and Eve, so he set out to destroy the creation of the early church with Ananias and Sapphira. *(Lockyer, p. 152)*

Where had they gone wrong, and how did it begin? How could they have witnessed such supernatural events and still considered carrying forth their diabolical scheme? "... Sapphira and her husband had become more interested in what they had than in what they were." *(Deen, p. 216)* Thus, we witness the "first defection in the church." *(McGee, Vol. 4, p. 530)*

The Instigator   (Acts 4:32-37; 5:1-5)

Instead of a welfare program, the early church adopted a plan to help their needy Christian friends. The Scriptures tell us a multitude of people believed and "had all things common." The early believers sold their lands and houses, bringing their money into the congregation and allowing the apostles to distribute it. No one lacked! Barnabas had just demonstrated his total self-sacrifice by selling his land and giving all of the money to the apostles. Can't you just hear the people? "Wow, look what Barnabas did! What a great man, so unselfish and giving!"

Perhaps wishing to emulate Barnabas and win favor with the congregation, Ananias and his wife Sapphira sold a certain possession. It evidently brought a good sum of money, so good that they decided to keep some back for themselves for a rainy day. Perhaps it was something they revered or idolized. However, their motives were not the same as those of Barnabas. They were double-minded, wanting to do good, wanting to impress others, but also wanting to protect themselves in case this new movement fell through. Satan took advantage of that double-mindedness.

Ananias tied his money bag to his waist and set out for the church. He put the money bag at Peter's feet, making Peter believe it was the entire amount received. He wanted to be recognized as a saint without living a holy life. Discerning Peter boldly confronted Ananias and asked him why he had conceived in his heart to lie? Here we find the sin began with a heart issue. Peter likewise told him he had lied unto God, not to men. The sin was not in keeping back part of the money. Peter said, "Whiles it remained, was it not thine own?" It was in the lying! Peter revealed three things to Ananias:

1. The origin of his sin – Satan
2. The sin itself – Lying to the Holy Spirit
3. The aggravations of the sin – Ananias was under no obligation to sell the land or to give the money.
(Henry, Vol. VI, p. 54)

God's judgment was swift with no further discussion, and Ananias dropped over dead. Henry states, "It is often of fatal consequence for people to go a great length in profession than their inward principle will admit of." *(Henry, Vol. VI, p. 54)*

What an object lesson to the congregation as great fear overtook them! The young men arose and carried him out of the congregation. God divided the tares from the wheat.

The Accomplice   (Acts 5:6-11)

Three hours later, Sapphira, "not knowing what was done, came in." Did she possess better character than her husband? How much had they connived? Would she lie about the selling price, too?

Peter, in holy wisdom, confronted her also. He said, "How much did you receive for the sale of your land? Now we are finally told exactly what they had sold – their land! Sapphira cast about in her mind what to say. Without giving it a lot of thought and remembering what she and Ananias had discussed, she quoted Peter the same amount Ananias had disclosed.

Peter asked her, "How could you both have agreed to tempt the Lord?" Sapphira could have taken a stand and told the truth. Remember, every man must give account of himself to the Lord. *(Rom. 14:12)* However, she persisted in carrying out the scheme, reaping dire consequences. **Note:** God did not excuse her sin because she submitted to her husband's scheme! She was responsible for her own actions. Submission was no cover-up!

In fact, it is possible that the entire plot was her idea! Perhaps she had convinced Ananias that they had worked hard for what they had and needed to keep back a "nest egg."

Peter told her the same men who had carried her dead husband out would carry her out also. She had no time to repent, no time to say good-bye to her loved ones, and no time to change her mind. The deed was done! She, too, dropped dead! Ananias and Sapphira literally lived out James 1:14-15:

> But every man is tempted, when he is drawn away of his own lust, and enticed. Then when lust hath conceived, it bringeth forth sin: and sin, when it is finished, bringeth forth death.

The first purging of the early church had taken place. Talk about church discipline! Great fear overtook the whole church and everyone who heard about it!

Results

Yes, great fear, dread, and awe fell upon the early church. It was their first episode of church discipline and one they would never forget! However, after the inner purging, we find great signs and wonders taking place with great multitudes turning to Christ. Scripture reveals, ". . . they were all with one accord in Solomon's porch." Unity had been restored. The inner purging brought revival, and Peter had more power upon his life than ever before. The early believers learned first hand that pride goes before a fall.

Conclusions

Why didn't Sapphira use her power of influence to persuade her husband against such an act? It appears that she was as carnal as he, and they together connived the scheme. As Peter said, "How is it that ye have agreed **together** to tempt the Spirit of the Lord?" *(Acts 5:9)*

What a warning to us as ladies this should be to willingly stand alone for the Higher Authority in our lives! As Christians, we each have a duty and obligation to obey the Word of God. At the judgment seat of Christ, we will stand alone to be judged for our works. What are you building on your foundation – wood, hay and stubble, or gold, silver, and precious stones? First Corinthians 3:13 says, "Every man's work shall be made manifest: for the day shall declare it, because it shall be revealed by fire: and the fire shall try every man's work of what sort it is."

We see the same situations in our local churches of today. Many have witnessed people getting saved and baptized. They have heard the Word rightly divided with powerful preaching. They have witnessed great events in their own local church, yet they hold back or lie to the Holy Spirit. It is a heart issue which needs to be addressed! They try to make others believe their all has been surrendered, but they continue to hold grudges, evil thoughts, and other sinful attitudes in their hearts. Lockyer pictures it perfectly:

> They wanted to give the impression that their all was on the altar, when it was not, and thus they became guilty of sacrilege in the attempt to obtain the reputation of saintliness with the reality of sacrifice. *(Lockyer, p. 153)*

Dear lady, are you a modern day Sapphira? Do you look saintly on the outside but have a heart full of deceit? Do you connive with other carnal ladies and gossip, causing division and strife in your church family? Do you pass on things you know are not verified as being true? If so, shame on you! Reflect on the goodness of the Lord and what He has done in and through your church. Clear your mind of evil thoughts and cleanse your heart of evil intent. Recharge your spiritual batteries on the Word of God and prayer. Make your sincere apologies and restitutions, and make a fresh start.

Are you trusting in a web of deceit and carnality? The web you weave will not stand. Job 8:13-15 aptly describes Sapphira:

> So are the paths of all that forget God; and the hypocrite's hope shall perish: Whose hope shall be cut off, and whose trust shall be a spider's web. He shall lean upon his house, but it shall not stand: he shall hold it fast, but it shall not endure.

Sapphira held fast to her web of deceit, but it did not withstand God's scrutiny. Remember, you can hide nothing from your omniscient and omnipotent God. He will not tolerate hypocrisy and lying. **"Be sure your sin will find you out!"**

Sapphira's Roles   Sapphira's Character Traits

1. Wife
2. Accomplice
3. Liar
4. Hypocrite
5. Schemer
6. Seller
7. Giver

1. Deceit
2. Carnality
3. Pride
4. Double-mindedness
5. Greed

Chapter 10

DRUSILLA
&
BERNICE

"Two Sisters Who Hated One Another"

Facts

Drusilla:

Husband:	Felix
Children:	Agrippa
Occupation:	First Lady
Her name means:	"Watered by the dew"

Bernice:

Husband:	Herod Agrippa II
Children:	Unknown
Occupation:	First Lady
Her name means:	"Victorious, "Carrying off victory"

Background

Both of these ladies lived during the era of the early church and were aware of the religious awakening taking place. Both were First Ladies, both were immoral, and both refused to recognize their need for Christ. Although they were privileged to hear the greatest apostle who ever lived, the great orator Paul, both shrugged off any conviction and pursued their sinful ways.

Their names? Drusilla and Bernice, biological sisters who hated one another.

Family Ties

We see a similar theme in Drusilla's life to that of Herodias'. Both were married to men of power and were in an adulterous relationship. Both were stolen from other men and admired for their great beauty.

Drusilla was the baby daughter of Herod Agrippa I. The Herod family was known for its clandestine affairs, jealousy, and treachery. Close family ties did not exist for them. Power, prestige, and pursuit of happiness filled their days and was applauded. Drusilla's father had killed the Apostle James, her great uncle had killed John the Baptist, and her great-grandfather attempted to kill Christ. No price was too great to obtain and keep power!

Historical accounts affirm that Drusilla married King Aziz at a young age after he had become a Jew. Living up to her family's reputation, she forsook him for Felix, the Roman procurator of Judea, and moved up the political ladder.

Fatal Exposure   (Acts 24)

Tertullus, a great orator of the day, carried a blasphemous, accusatory report to Felix concerning Paul. He called Paul a seditionist and a cultist, using religious terms and the Jews' name to sound more plausible. Felix permitted Paul to defend himself. God gave Felix and Drusilla a chance to be saved! "Their palace becomes a church and their thrones become almost a mourner's bench." *(McGee, p. 620)*

After hearing Paul's defense, Felix was reluctant to make a rash decision, saying he would wait until the chief captain came to hear more. He confined Paul, but granted him liberty for visitors.

Carnal and Conniving
Women of the Bible, volume 5

After a few days, Felix sent for Paul again, this time in the presence of his wife Drusilla. Had Drusilla, a Jewess herself, encouraged Felix to call for Paul again? Perhaps curiosity motivated her to seek an audience with Paul. Paul rose to the occasion and boldly witnessed to them of Christ. As he spoke of "righteousness, temperance, and judgment," Felix began to tremble. It was not the message either one expected! They were well aware of their lustful, sinful lifestyle, and Paul "laid the axe to the root."

Seeking to shrug off the conviction, Felix dismissed Paul, saying he would call for him at a "more convenient time." For two years, Paul remained bound, although Felix communed with him often. We do not see Drusilla encouraging her husband to make a decision for the Lord or ever seeking to be in Paul's presence again. Paul had exposed her private sins, and she was not happy! Unlike Felix, she did not tremble, although she was equally guilty. Henry likens her to many who have a curiosity about religion – they "can be content to have their judgments informed but not their lives reformed." *(Henry, Vol. VI, p. 314)*

Alexander Whyte suspects her of urging Felix to send Paul back to prison and "cutting short the discourse."

Lockyer adds,

> My belief about the royal pair is, that had Drusilla not sat beside Felix that day, Felix would have been baptized, and Paul would have been set free, before the sun had gone down. But Drusilla and her sisters have cast into their graves many wounded. Many strong men have been slain to death by them. Their house is the way to hell, and their steps go down to the chambers of death. *(Lockyer, p. 49)*

This theory seems entirely plausible, as we see Drusilla exhibit no further interest in hearing Paul. Felix communed with him and hoped someone would give money to release him. Perhaps Drusilla was concerned about her royal position and her security.

She is a picture of the strange woman mentioned in Proverbs, and refused to allow her life to be "watered by the dew" of God's Word.

Nothing more is heard of Drusilla, and tradition holds that nearly twenty years later, she, along with her son Agrippa, died in the eruption of Vesuvius in Pompeii. Paul's prophecy of "judgment to come" came to pass in her life.

> Drusilla, who had dishonored her faith, rejected the
> preaching of Christ, forsaken her husband, and lived
> on in sinful wedlock – that Drusilla, learned how awful
> it is to fall into the hand of a living God. *(Kuyper, p. 106)*

Instant Replay   (Acts 25:23 - 26:28)

Two short years later, we see the story re-enacted in the lives of Agrippa and Bernice. Bernice was the oldest daughter of Herod Agrippa I. Great jealousy had always existed between her and Drusilla. Drusilla was the pretty one, the baby. Bernice was plainer in looks, but knew how to obtain and wield power.

Bernice had been married many times. A man named Marcus and her uncle Herod were the first two men in her life. Like Drusilla, she lived in an immoral relationship. Her lustful deeds included incest with her own brother, Herod Agrippa II. What terrible role models these women were for leadership positions!

Since Paul had already appealed to Caesar, he was not required by law to appear before Herod. However, he seized upon the opportunity to once again boldly present the gospel.

Agrippa and Bernice looked forward to the dispute. Along with chief captains and important men of the city, they met with Paul. Scripture tells us that they entered with great pomp. Bernice was used to attention and had no shame of public appearances.

Agrippa granted Paul permission to make his defense. Paul gave personal testimony of his conversion and asked Agrippa if he believed the prophets. Agrippa uttered the well-known statement, "Almost thou persuadest me to be a Christian." *(Acts 26:28)*

We see Bernice making no effort to influence her husband to free Paul. The only record of Bernice's thoughts is her recognition that Paul was not worthy of death. *(Acts 26:31)* Her lust and love of prestige hindered her from seizing the golden opportunity Paul presented.

Future Scandal

The annals of history record Bernice's continued decadence. She later married King Ptolemy of Sicily, but tired of him and returned to her brother again. Her continual pursuit of sensuality led to an immoral relationship with Titus, the Roman Emperor from A.D. 79-81 who destroyed Jerusalem. Her seared conscience resulted in a reprobate mind spoken of in Romans one. Although she heard one of the greatest orators of all time, she continued on in her lifestyle, exhibiting no fear of God or desire to serve Him.

Conclusions

What a vivid portrait of sin we see in these ladies' lives. They are comparable to Jezebel, Herodias, and Athaliah. Their pursuit for this world's goods, sensual lusts, power, and prestige hindered them from believing on the only One Who could bring total contentment and satisfaction.

Felix trembled, and Agrippa was almost persuaded, yet their women showed no emotional response to the gospel. They loved their sin!

> The reason why sinners are not persuaded is, in ninety-nine cases out of a hundred, their sin, their love of sin!
> . . .Most of the arguments against the gospel are bred in the filth of a corrupt life."   *(Spurgeon, p. 865)*

Carnal and Conniving
Women of the Bible, volume 5

We can contrast these two women to Esther who influenced her husband to save a nation, to Pilate's wife who urged her husband to find no fault with the just man, and to the queen of Sheba, who traveled to a far country to find the good news and share it with her own people.

Ladies, we **can** live pure and clean lives. Our past does not matter! God forgives all sin and wipes the slate clean.

Drusilla and Bernice were two shameless women sharing similar lifestyles, and two stubborn ladies who refused God's perfect gift for their lives! May the same never be said of us!

> The foolish atheist says, "There is no God." The foolish Christian says, "No, God! You cannot have your way in my life; I will do as I please." It is a dangerous thing to say "No, God!" When you shut God out of your life, your conscience becomes hardened. You may do corrupt and abominable things you never thought you could do. It is also dangerous because "it is a fearful thing to fall into the hands of the living God." (Hebrews 10:31)
>
> *(Purcell, p. 154)*

Drusilla's Roles

1. Wife
2. Adulteress
3. First Lady
4. Strange woman
5. Mother

Drusilla's Character Traits

1. Immorality
2. Hard-heartedness
3. Curiosity
4. Worldliness

Bernice's Roles

1. Wife
2. Fornicator
3. Queen
4. Strange woman

Bernice's Character Traits

1. Immorality
2. Selfishness
3. Pride
4. Greed

70

Sources

Briscoe, Jill. *Women Who Changed Their World.* Wheaton: SP Publications, Inc., 1991.

Chappell, Clovis G. *Feminine Faces.* Nashville: Abingdon-Cokesbury Press (Whitmore & Stone), 1942.

Davis Dictionary of the Bible. Nashville: Royal Publishers, Inc., 1973.

Deen, Edith. *All of the Women of the Bible.* New York: Harper and Row Publishers, 1955.

Deen, Edith. *Wisdom From Women in the Bible.* San Francisco: Harper and Row Publishers, Inc., 1978.

Fallows, Samuel. *The Popular & Critical Bible Encyclopedia, Vol. I, II, and III.* Chicago: The Howard-Severance Company, 1907.

Feature, A Daily Bible Study Guide (Oct-Dec, 2002). Los Osos, California: Fundamental EvangelisticAssociation: 2002.

George, Elizabeth. *The Remarkable Women of the Bible.* Eugene, Oregon: Harvest House Publishers, 2003.

George, Elizabeth. *Women Who Loved God.* Eugene, Oregon: Harvest House Publishers, 1999.

Handford, Elizabeth Rice. *Profiles of Genesis Women.* Chattanooga: Joyful Christian Ministries, 1991.

Handford, Elizabeth Rice. *Women in the Wilderness.* Chattanooga: Joyful Christian Ministries, 1992.

Handford, Elizabeth Rice. *Women Under the Judges.* Chattanooga: Joyful Christian Ministries, 1993.

Sources (continued)

Handford, Elizabeth Rice. *Women Under the Kings.* Chattanooga: Joyful Christian Ministries, 1995.

Harrison, Everett F. and Charles F. Pfeiffer. ed. *Wycliffe Commentary.* Chicago: The Moody Bible Institute, 1962.

Henry, Matthew. *Matthew Henry's Commentary, Vol. I, II, V, and VI.* Fleming H. Revell Company.

Horton, Robert F. *Women of the Old Testament.* London: Service and Paton, 1899.

Jensen, Mary E. *Bible Women Speak to Us Today.* Minneapolis: Augsburg Publishing House, 1983.

Jones, Beneth Peters. *The Wilderness Within.* Greenville: Bob Jones University Press, 2002.

Karssen, Gien. *Her Name is Woman, Books 1 & 2.* Colorado Springs: Navpress, 1991.

Kuyper, Abraham. *Women of the New Testament.* Grand Rapids: Zondervan Publishing House, 1934 (renewed 1962).

Lockyer, Herbert. *All the Women of the Bible.* Grand Rapids: Zondervan Publishing House.

Matheson, George. *Portraits of Bible Women.* Grand Rapids: Kregel Publications, 1986.

McAllister, Grace. *God Portrays Women.* Chicago: Moody Press, 1954.

McGee, J. Vernon. *Through the Bible With J. Vernon McGee Vol. 1, 2 and 4.* Nashville: Thomas Nelson, Inc., 1981.

Morton, H.V. *Women of the Bible.* New York: Dodd, Mead, and Company, 1941.

Nave, Orville J. *Nave's Topical Bible.* McLean, Virginia: MacDonald Publishing Company.

Nelson, Thomas. (Gen. ed.). *The King James Study Bible for Women.* Thomas Nelson, Inc., 2003.

Orr, James. *The International Standard Bible Encyclopedia.* Grand Rapids: Wm. B. Erdman's Publishing Co., 1939, 1956.

Poole, Matthew. *A Commentary on the Holy Bible, Vol. I and III.* McLean, Virginia: MacDonald Publishing Company.

Price, Eugenia. *God Speaks to Women Today.* Grand Rapids: Zondervan Publishing House, 1964.

Price, Eugenia. *The Unique World of Women.* Grand Rapids: Zondervan Publishing House, 1969.

Purcell, Juanita. *Be Still, My Child.* Schaumburg, Illionis: Regular Baptist Press, 1997.

Rice, John R. *Genesis.* Murfreesboro: Sword of the Lord Publishers, 1975.

Ryrie, Charles Caldwell. *The Ryrie Study Bible.* Chicago: Moody Press, 1978.

Spurgeon, Charles H. *The Treasury of the Bible, Vol. I.* Grand Rapids: Baker Book House, 1988.

Tenney, Merrill, C. (Gen. ed.). *Pictorial Bible Dictionary.* Nashville: The Southwestern Company, 1974.

Unger, Merrill F. *The New Unger's Bible Dictionary.* Chicago: Moody Press, 1988.

Sources (continued)

Vine, W.E., Merrill F. Unger, and William White, Jr. *Vine's Expository Dictionary of Biblical Words.* Nashville, Camden, New York: Thomas Nelson Publishers, 1985. in America, 1954.

Webster's Dictionary. Miami: P.S. I. Associates, 1986 ed

Wiersbe, Warren. *Through The Year.* Grand Rapids: Baker Books, 1999.

Zodhiates, Spiros, Th.D. *The Complete Word Study New Testament.* Chattanooga: AMG Publishers, 1991.

DISCLAIMER: Inclusion of an author or his quote does not mean that we endorse that author's ministry, doctrinal position, or his writings (including that book).